BASS BUILDERS

RON CARTER

BUILDING JAZZ BASS LINES

ISBN 978-0-7935-8634-9

HAL•LEONARD®
CORPORATION

7777 W. BLUEMOUND RD. P.O. BOX 13819 MILWAUKEE, WI 53213

Visit Hal Leonard Online at
www.halleonard.com

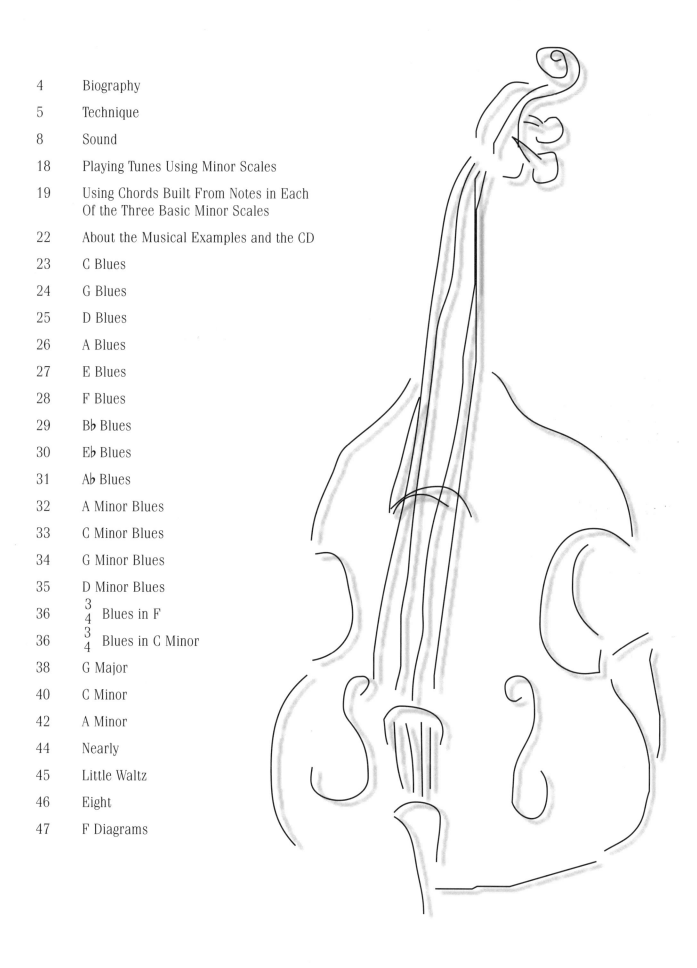

4   Biography

5   Technique

8   Sound

18 Playing Tunes Using Minor Scales

19 Using Chords Built From Notes in Each
    Of the Three Basic Minor Scales

22 About the Musical Examples and the CD

23 C Blues

24 G Blues

25 D Blues

26 A Blues

27 E Blues

28 F Blues

29 B♭ Blues

30 E♭ Blues

31 A♭ Blues

32 A Minor Blues

33 C Minor Blues

34 G Minor Blues

35 D Minor Blues

36 $\frac{3}{4}$ Blues in F

36 $\frac{3}{4}$ Blues in C Minor

38 G Major

40 C Minor

42 A Minor

44 Nearly

45 Little Waltz

46 Eight

47 F Diagrams

Biography

Ron Carter is one of the most important bass players/leaders/composers in jazz. Born in Michigan in 1937, he originally took up the cello at the age of ten, with the intention of playing classical music. At 17, he took up the bass. He attended the Eastman School of Music, receiving his Bachelor of Music degree in 1959. He went to New York, played with the Chico Hamilton Quintet, and enrolled at the Manhattan School of Music, where he earned his Masters degree in 1961. After leaving the Hamilton group, he freelanced in New York, where he not only played with Don Ellis, Randy Weston, Thelonious Monk and Art Farmer, but played numerous television and recording dates. In 1963, he joined Miles Davis's quintet and stayed until 1968. It is generally acknowledged that this ensemble, with Wayne Shorter, Herbie Hancock and Tony Williams, was not only one of Davis's finest groups, it was one of the most important jazz groups in the history of the music. The band recorded several albums and toured all over the world.

While continuing to be one of the most in-demand bassists for recording sessions of all types, he has led many groups of his own to worldwide acclaim. Carter introduced the piccolo bass (an instrument one half the size of the regular acoustic bass) so that he could stand out as the leader of his ensembles.

He has appeared on thousands of albums as either rhythm section player, composer, arranger and/or producer. His compositions include the Grammy winning "Call Street Blues," featured in the motion picture *Round Midnight.* He is the author of several books on bass technique, and is a respected and popular teacher, currently Distinguished Professor of Music at City College of New York. Students have come from all over the world to study with a master of the instrument and a brilliant accompanist, celebrated for his flawless time and harmonically and rhythmically rich lines.

Technique

One of the problems facing the young bassist is how to play fast tempos—(which method to use— alternating fingers, right hand, one finger, two fingers, etc.) I have designed some right-hand exercises to assist the bassist since there are several approaches to this problem. The exercises are to be done quite slowly at first to obtain the best sound and the longest notes possible, gradually increasing tempos, still listening for long notes and good sound. At the height of the tempo, accelerate. Be sure that the notes are as long and the sounds as good as they were at the beginning of the exercise.

The first exercise "A" shows the speed exercise using stationary fingers (see photo). It is important to be sure that once the right hand has played the notes on the G string that the hand goes immediately to the D string as in the form of a slur with the bow, without using the bow. It is equally important to remember that when the right hand goes from the D to the G string, the hand be kept as close to the strings as possible to facilitate the feel for the G string and the developing of a "touch" for all strings on up-tempo tunes.

Exercise A

strings: D A D A D A D A

The next exercise has the right hand alternating fingers, e.g. 1-2-1-2. Again, as in the previous exercise, the starting tempo should be slow enough to combine good sound and long notes with the coordinating and alternating of the first and second fingers.

Note:
When alternating fingers, the fingers should be kept as close to the strings when the fingers are not being used as when they are being used. The two sets of numbers in this exercise are intended for the right hand only, not to be confused with the left-hand technique.

The following exercises are designed to aid the bassist in gaining speed crossing three strings, then jumping a string. The exercises should be played with a consistent tempo. After completing each exercise, repeat the exercise faster than before (sans accel.) to develop coordination and rhythm between the right and left hand, keeping in mind the importance of good sound and long notes.

Note: The third note of each measure is marked with a –, and should be particularly long to facilitate the playing of the next note.

The high degree of coordination between fingered left-hand notes and fingered right-hand notes (or strings being played on) is of the utmost importance and primary aim of the next exercise. The same practice instructions given to the preceding exercises are to be applied here. The two sets of numbers again apply to the right hand.

Note:
The fingered notes of this exercise are those of the G Major scale, therefore no left-hand fingering is necessary.

Here's essentially, the same exercise alternates the fingers of the right hand. This should be played slowly to insure the playing of the note with the left hand and the plucking of the same note with the finger indicated on the right hand occurring precisely at the same time.

Note:

The order of notes are all located across the instrument, hence, horizontal playing. In this and the preceding exercise, the right-hand numbers are 2, 1 rather than 1, 2. This is to achieve a longer sound on each 8 note phrase.

The following exercise has the bassist doing a speed exercise crossing four strings. Note the right hand, when playing the ascending passage, stays close to the strings at all times and when it is playing the descending passage, the right hand plays with one motion, hence, the ⟶ arrow. The entire exercise must be done slowly at first, then gradually increase the tempo until the desired speed is attained.

Note:

The numbers in the exercise are for the left hand only.

Sound

Why do some bassists have "longer" notes than others? Why do some have a more consistent sound than others? And why do some have a better projection of sound than others? Many answers can be found in the placing and positioning of the right hand (the "picking" hand) on the instrument. The photo and following exercises (if observed and practiced carefully and, diligently) will do a great deal and go a long way toward eliminating many problems in attaining the previously mentioned achievement levels.

Using the picture to be sure your right hand is in the proper position, practice the following exercises. Start each exercise slowly at first, gradually increase the tempo, then gradually ritard.

Limiting the blues line to one position (half-position), below is an example chart of half position showing the notes, the string on which they are played, and the proper fingering for each note.

By playing in a position (in this case half-position) as long as possible, or playing across the instrument (horizontally, I call it), you are assured of more consistent pitch, more combinations of notes, and a more consistent level of good tone.

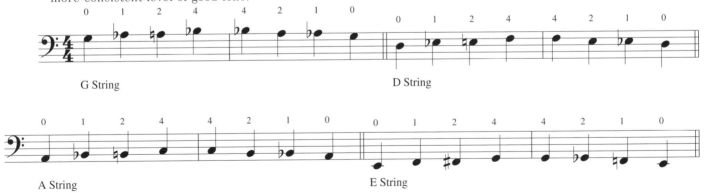

To illustrate how a good bass line is developed, I have taken a 12-bar blues progression, which is probably the first form of improvisation with which the student will have contact, from the basic chord spelling to the use of *non-harmonic* notes to the use of *rhythm*. These last two terms are described in detail further along in the text.

The first line is an example of a basic blues progression using the basic chord per bar.

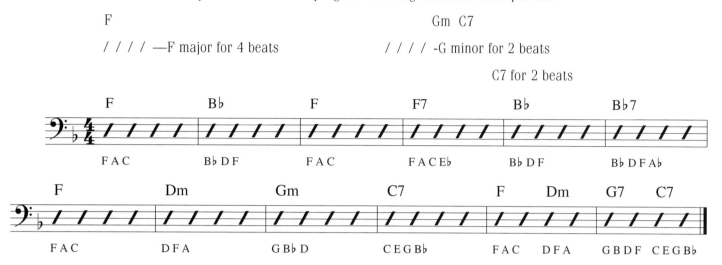

Letters below the staff show the proper spelling of each chord.

Here is a chart of the more common symbols, what they mean, and how they affect the chord spelling.

The m means minor; the chord being built on a minor and major third—D to F to A—DFA.

The 7 means a seventh (dominant) is to be added to the chord spelling—D7—DF♯A + C—DF♯AC.

The Maj7 means a major seventh has been added to the chord spelling Dmaj7—DFA + C♯—DFAC♯.

The o means the chord is built on minor thirds DFA♭, and is called a diminished chord.

The + means that the chord is built on two major triads DF♯ A♯, and is called an augmented chord.

The diagram below shows only two of the many possibile combinations of notes played in half-position, using the chords F and B♭. It is not necessary for the first note of every measure to be the root or tonic of the chord.

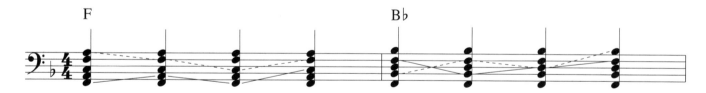

Here we have one possible combination of the blues form, with the proper fingering, using the basic chord progression, the proper chord spelling of that chord progression, and limiting ourselves to half-position.

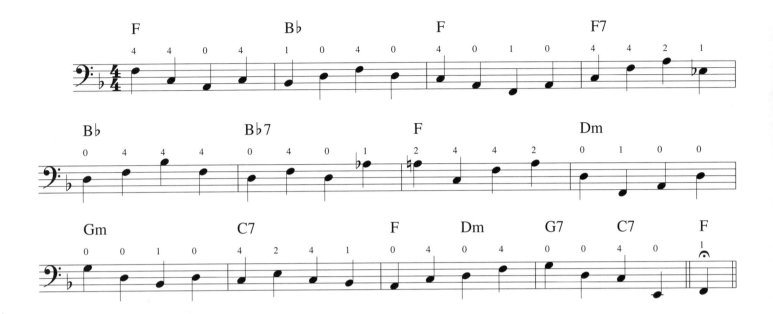

Referring to the original blues progression, we will now add what is known as *non-harmonic* material, or notes that are not a part of the original chord spelling. Note that the ( ) indicates which note has been replaced. Notice that the addition of the *non-harmonic* notes does not bring about any necessity for any position change

Now we are ready to add another dimension to the progression by adding rhythm, sometimes known as *fills*, to replace the 4-quarter-note pattern. Rhythm can be used to emphasize a particular note, a group of notes, a different chord progression, or a *vamp* (the repeating of a particular note phrase over a certain chord or group of chords).

You should be careful not to overdo the use of rhythm patterns for fear that the feeling of a "walking bass line" be destroyed. Your personal tastes and judgment will govern this area of your playing.

In the bass line below, we have analyzed each non-harmonic note as if it were an extension of the basic chord. For example: Dm9 is now spelled D, F, A, C, E, rather than D, F, A.

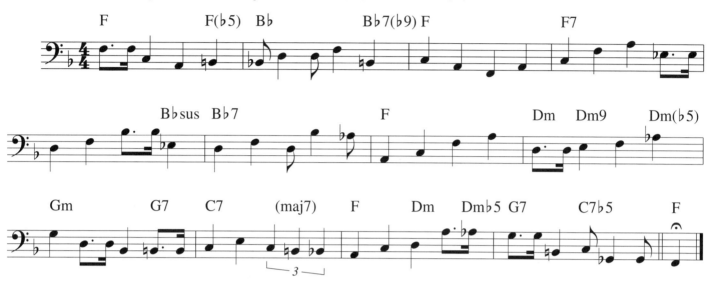

In the bass line below, we have analyzed the progression with the non-harmonic notes serving as a note in an altered or substitute chord—those chords that will function as a substitute or replacement for the original chord used at that particular spot in the progression.

Even the seventh can function as a note of another chord.

*Note the enharmonic spelling of E♭ (D♯) in the B7.
+Note the enharmonic spelling of B♮ (C♭) in the D♭7.

Horizontal bass playing means the playing and developing of lines on the instrument in a given position without shifting (vertical playing). While some shifting of position will be inevitable, the least amount of position shifts that can be affected leads to better sound and better time. All of the notes are more conveniently located producing better and larger choices of notes due to the playing across the instrument's four strings rather than up and down one or two strings.

Using the basic blues progression shown here, I have illustrated and analyzed how this concept should be approached. The exercise employs only the 7th position. As we begin our study of this method, you will notice that the numbers over the notes designate how to finger each note, and occasionally beneath certain notes, you will find the proper string on which to play this particular note or group of notes.

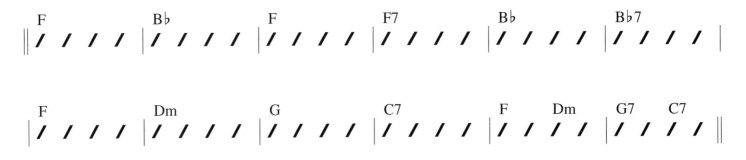

Note:
This exercise should be played very slowly to fully grasp this horizontal concept and to facilitate and coordinate the crossing of strings with the left and right hand.

Now we see how the original blues line can be altered by replacing a few notes with what I call *non-harmonic tones* or notes that are not a part of the original chord spelling. The substitution of these notes does not make shifting positions necessary while adding another dimension to the line. The original notes are in ( ) so a comparison between the two notes is immediately obvious. The new note is fingered such that the horizontal concept is maintained.

In the following exercise we show how we can increase the range of the instrument as we stay in position by the careful adding of the open string, notated by the X located under the particular note. It is important to make the note length of the fingered or closed note match that of the open string note as closely as possible. Make the notes marked X have the same sound blend or weight, not the open string loud and strong and the fingered note weak and anemic. In comparing the basic blues exercise to this one, you will notice how the substitution of an open string for a fingered note not only increases the harmonic possibilities of the chord, but also the range of the instrument in this position and makes the horizontal theory even more applicable.

Note:
This exercise should be played slowly and deliberately to blend the two sounds and to practice left-hand technique.

In this exercise we see the use of open strings played with the non-harmonic tones. This adds another flavor to the line—the color of an open string sound with a non-harmonic tone and the original blues line. The bassist should be reminded here, as in the following example, that the sound and note length of the open string should match that of the closed or fingered note. The fingered note played before the open string note is held in place so the sound of that particular fingered note carries over to the next note. This is notated by the (⌒) between the two notes.

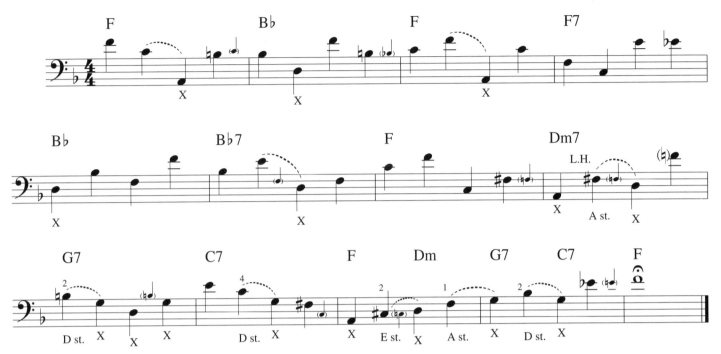

This bass line shows one possibility of playing rhythm while staying in position and using open strings. In bars 9 and 12 the notes G are to be played as one open and the following one closed or fingered. Make sure the figures are played with the correct rhythm and in the proper meter as illustrated in the text for the earlier rhythm exercise. Again it is important that each note played should have as good and as long a sound as is possible.

Here we see how rhythm is added as another device to the bass line thus, giving it still another flavor without destroying either the blues feeling or the walking bass-line concept. All of the dotted eighth note to sixteenth note passages  should be given their full values with as long a sound on the sixteenth note as possible while still playing horizontally.

The quarter note triplets should be played rhythmically properly within the bar and should be "felt" as the following metric figure:

The eighth note, dotted quarter note figure should be played without accent to avoid the eighth note from being played too late and the dotted quarter note from being played too soon.

Before you play your own version of the blues in F, I have supplied two sets of diagrams to be used as worksheets.

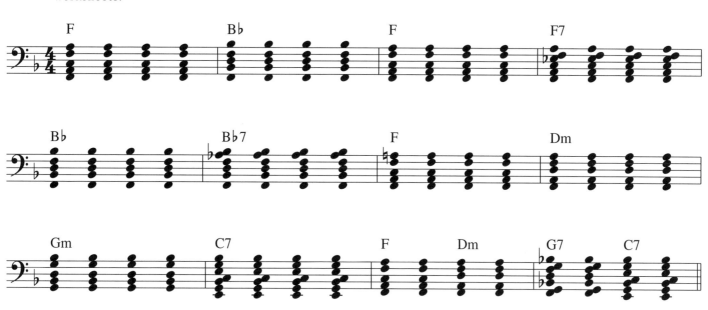

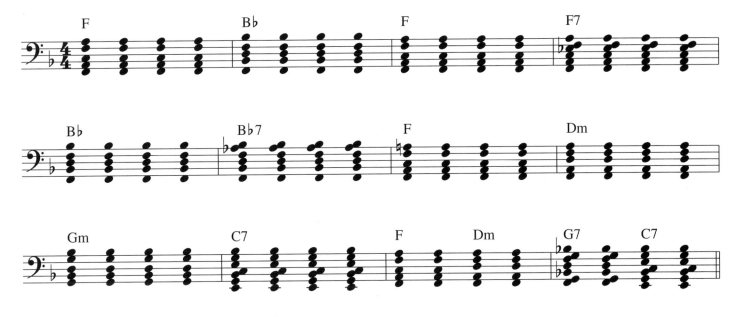

Additional diagrams in F may be found on pages 47 and 48.

With the advent of one or two-chord songs, e.g. "So What", "Why Not", the bassist is faced with how to sustain musical interest over a prolonged period of time using only these two chords.

Many concepts and possibilities of meeting this musical challenge are available. Below is among the many possibilities—a scale approach.

In this example with the key center of D Minor, we see how the D Minor scale, which is the relative minor of F Major, can be played. The example uses a "straight scale" type passage for the first four bars, a "broken scale" type for the second four bars, and a combination of the first two in the last four bars.

Using the scale theory we know three basic minor scales; natural, melodic and harmonic. It is quite interesting to see how the latter two minor scales add additional flavor to the one and two-chord tunes. This exercise shows a bass line built on the D melodic minor scale.

Note:
The melodic minor scale has altered notes on the sixth and seventh scale steps on the ascending passage and a lowered sixth and seventh scale steps (forming a natural minor scale) on the descending passage.

In the following bass line example we see the third possibility in the "scale theory"—this time using the harmonic minor scale.

Note:
The harmonic minor scale has altered notes on the seventh step of the ascending scale and this note alteration remains on the descending scale.

1. Playing Tunes Using Minor Scales

The following example illustrates another method of building a bass line on one and two-chord tunes—that of building chords based on each note in the D minor scale, either natural minor, melodic minor, or harmonic minor.

You will notice that the half notes outline a D natural minor scale, and the quarter notes represent notes that spell a particular chord.

Beneath the chord and scale illustration you will find a bass line built on this concept.

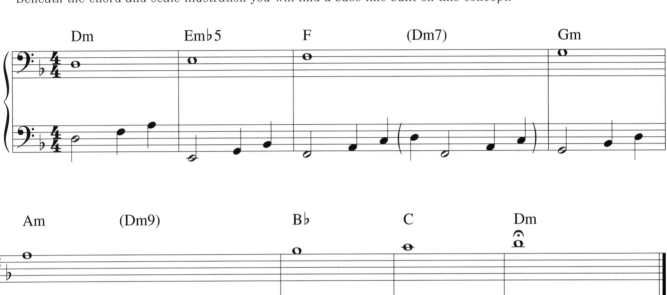

2. Using Chords Built From Notes In Each Of the Three Basic Minor Scales

Here we see the concept used in the previous bass line that dealt with the D natural minor scale is used below using the D melodic minor scale.

Since the descending part of the melodic minor is the same as the natural minor scale, I have illustrated chords for the ascending scale only.

Beneath the chord and scale illustration you will find a bass line built on this concept.

Finally, we see the concept used below applied to the third of the minor scales, the harmonic minor scale.

As in the preceding two minor scale examples, this one should be studied carefully to fully understand the basic theory behind the mechanics of the concept.

Thus far we have seen illustrations around playing one and two-chord tunes in two forms: 1.) playing these tunes by using minor scales, and 2.) by using chords built from notes in each of the three basic minor scales.

The third possibility in solving this problem is to create a chord progression with, in this case, a D Minor tonality.

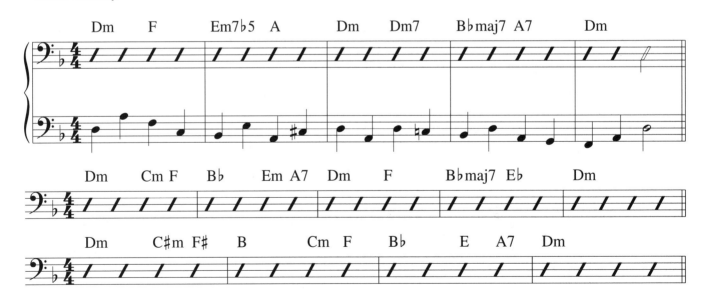

Note:
Here is an arbitrarily chosen set of chords in a D minor tonality with a corresponding bass line. As you can see, the possibilities are endless. I have written two additional sets of chords without bass lines. Study and experiment with these two lines to see the possibilities available to you.

An additional possibility for these types of tunes is to plan a vamp, or an ostinato bass line occurs at intervals designated by the bassist. Below, I have written a chord progression using a vamp that fits over these chords. Remember this is only one of many possibilities. Make your own and have a ball!

With regard to modal playing, there is no way to play four notes in a measure and have other musicians understand that these notes belong to the mode in question. I'd be interested to know if any of you has found a way to do this.

Good luck,

Ron Carter

About the Musical Examples and the CD

On the following pages are the musical examples as performed on the accompanying play-along CD. In playing situations, you may play in rhythm sections with piano, guitar and drums, guitar and drums, or piano and drums. The sounds and "feel" of these different situations dictate that several blues examples be given in a number of ways. Be sure to check the CD track to see the different rhythm combinations available.

The CD is made up of the following:

A.   Blues in major and minor keys

B.   3/4 Blues

C.   Blues examples in the three-step process described in the text. To review, they are:

1.   The basic bass line.
2.   A bass line with non-chord (non-harmonice) tones.
3.   A bass line with different rhythms added to the non-chord (non-harmonic) tones.

D.   Play-along rhythm sections for three of my compositions. The bass lines for the compositions are given here. For lead sheets of the compositions, see *The Ron Carter Collection*, also published by Hal Leonard (HL 00672331).

Special thanks to the musicians who performed on this CD. Besides myself they are:

Piano – Mulgrew Miller
Guitar – Ofer Ganor
Drums – Lewis Nash

Recorded at Avatar Studios, New York; Joe Ferla, recording engineer

C Blues

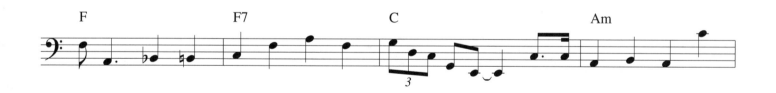

G Blues

D Blues

A Blues

E Blues

*Even though there is a G♯ in C♯ minor, the bass player still has G♮ as a note choice.

F Blues

B♭ Blues

Eb Blues

A♭ Blues

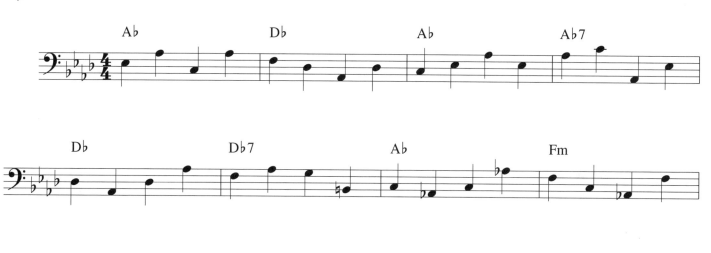

A Minor Blues

*Even though there is a C♮ in an F♯m♭5 chord, the bass player still has C♯ as a note choice.

C Minor Blues

G Minor Blues

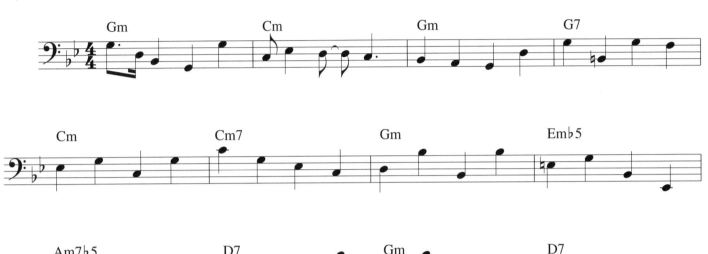

D Minor Blues

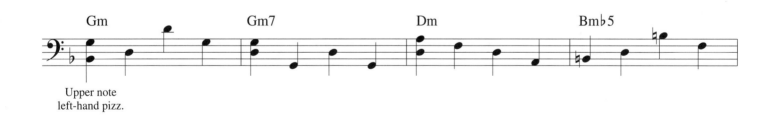

Upper note
left-hand pizz.

L.H.   L.H.

$\frac{3}{4}$ Blues in F

$\frac{3}{4}$ Blues in C Minor

Following are the blues examples in the three-step process. You will find a series of diagrams as on page 15. These diagrams represent the choices of the notes in the stated chord in a given position per beat. By connecting the notes from beat to beat through the examples, you not only see the choices of notes you have per beat per measure, but the shape of the line you are responsible for. The notes as connected represent the basic bass line that I play on the CD.

After the bass line with different rhythms added to the non-chord tones, I have included some diagrams for you to construct your own bass lines.

G Major

Bass Line Dots

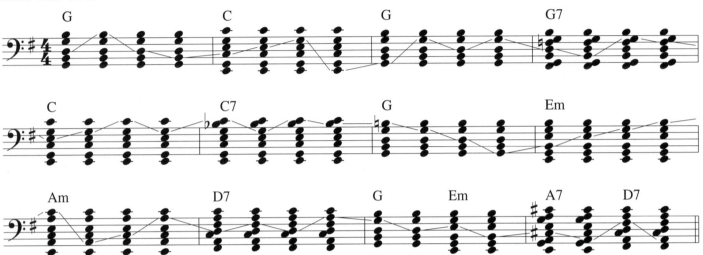

Basic Bass line

Bass Line with non-chord tones (or non-harmonic notes)

Bass line with different rhythms added to non-harmonic notes.

C Minor

Bass Line Dots

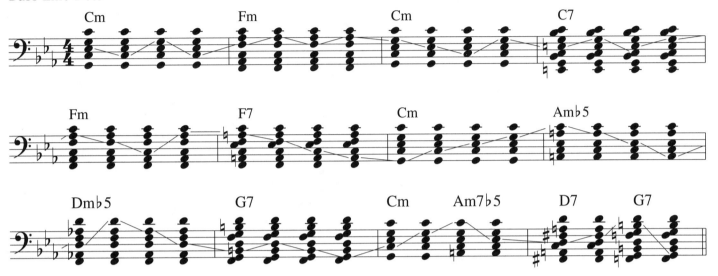

Basic Bass line

Bass Line with non-chord tones (or non-harmonic notes)

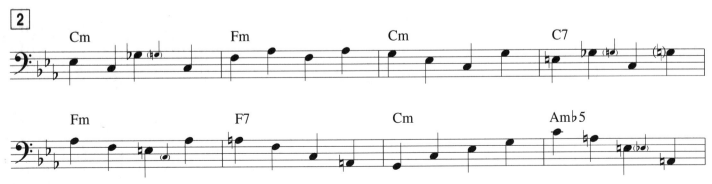

Bass line with different rhythms added to non-harmonic notes.

A Minor

Bass Line Dots

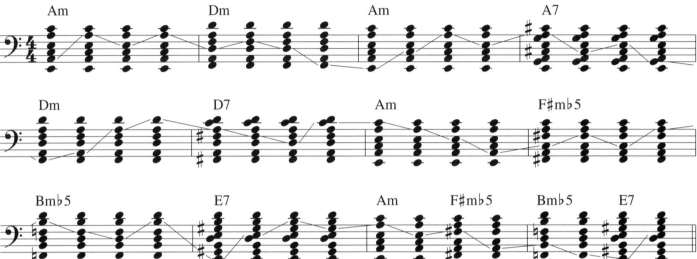

Basic Bass line

Bass Line with non-chord tones (or non-harmonic notes)

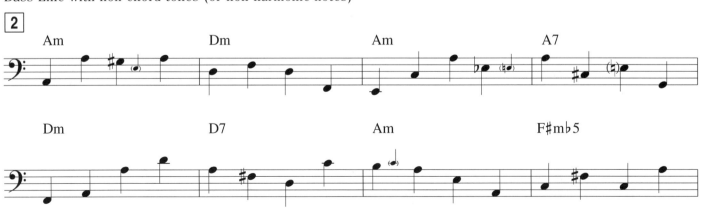

Bass line with different rhythms added to non-harmonic notes.

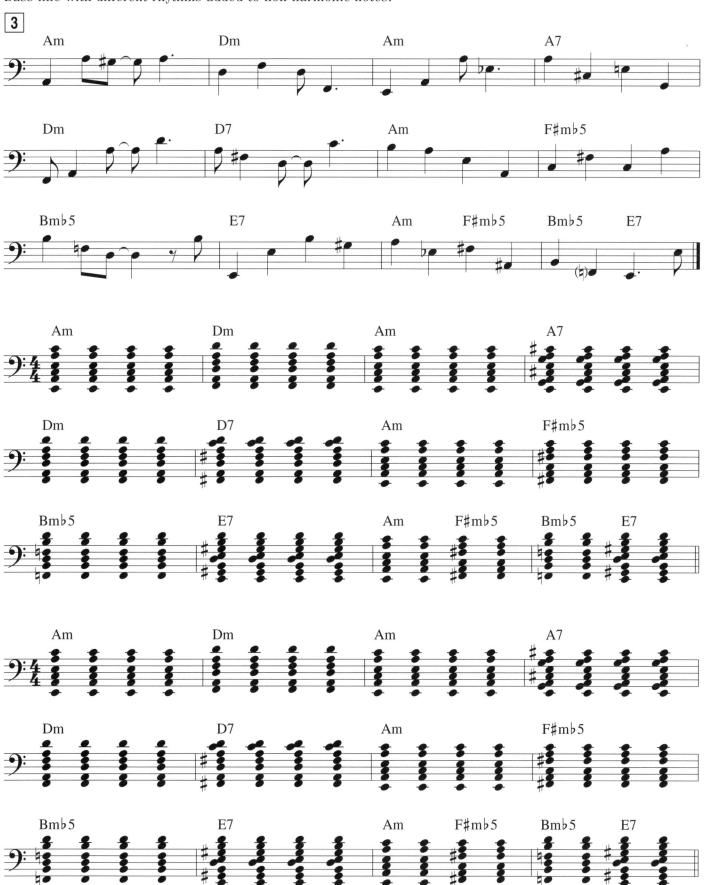

Nearly

By Ron Carter

Little Waltz

By Ron Carter

Eight

* For those bassists with extensions

F Diagrams

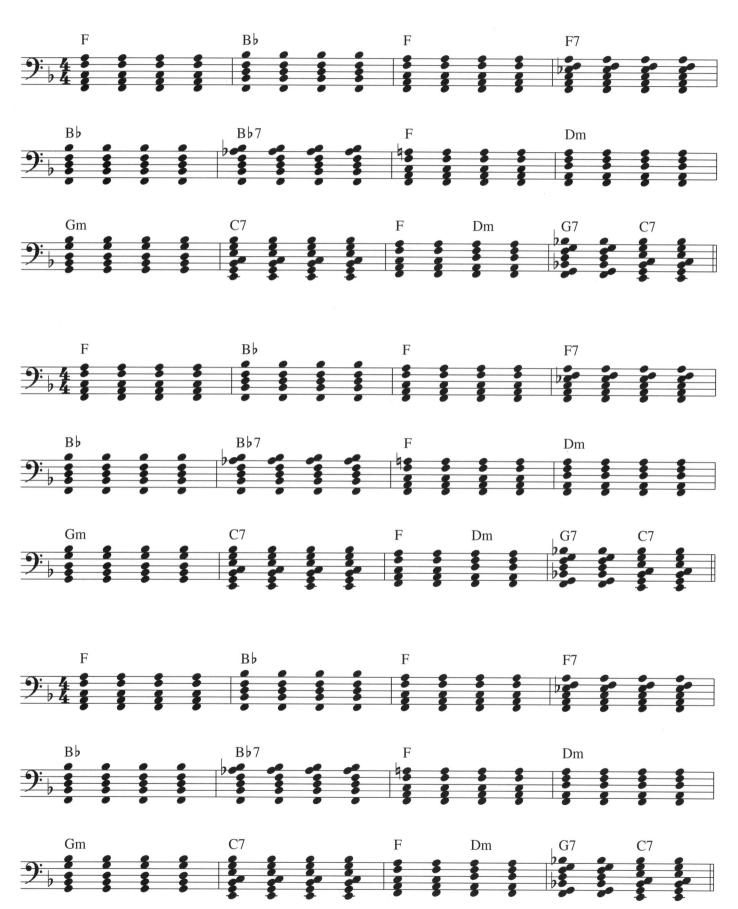

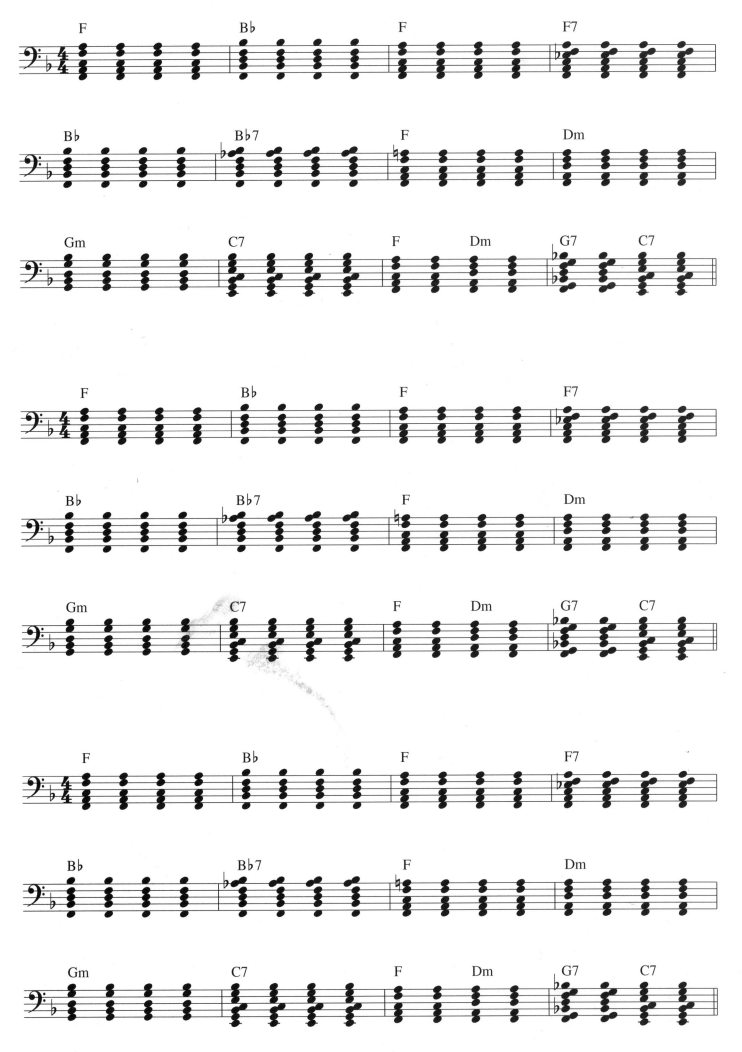